THANK YOU

For Purchasing This I Spy Valentine's Day Book For Kids

HAPPY Valentine's DAY

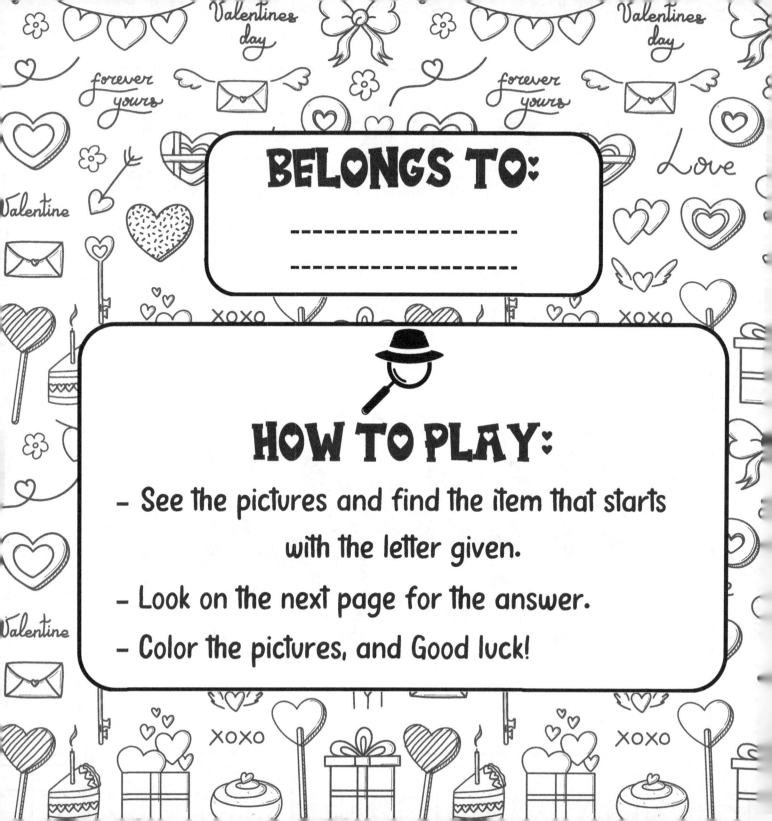

BELONGS TO:

HOW TO PLAY:

- See the pictures and find the item that starts with the letter given.

- Look on the next page for the answer.

- Color the pictures, and Good luck!

I spy With My Little Eye 🔍
Something Beginning With...

I spy With My Little Eye 🔍
Something Beginning With...

I spy With My Little Eye  Something Beginning With...

H

I spy With My Little Eye
Something Beginning With...

I

I spy With My Little Eye 🔍

Something Beginning With...

I spy With My Little Eye
Something Beginning With...

I spy With My Little Eye  Something Beginning With...

M

M

IT'S AN

COLOR ME!

Good JOB

MARRY

I spy With My Little Eye 🔍
Something Beginning With...

I spy With My Little Eye Something Beginning With...

I spy With My Little Eye 🔍
Something Beginning With...

Valentines day

U

IT'S A

COLOR ME!

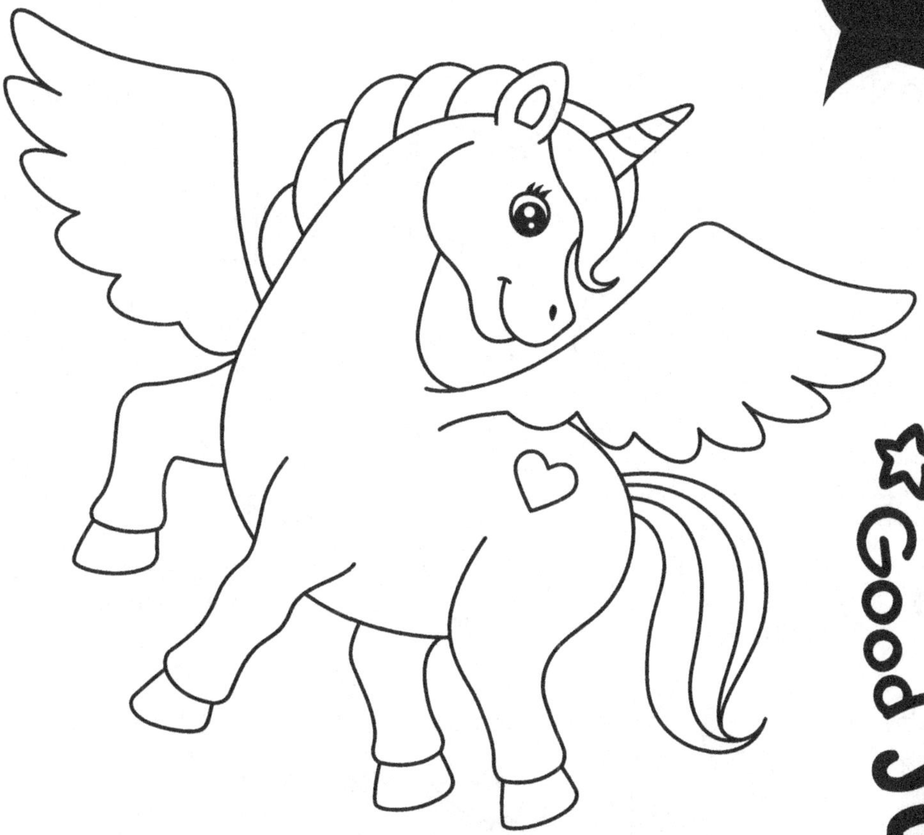

Good JOB

UNICORN

I spy With My Little Eye  Something Beginning With...

V

I spy With My Little Eye Something Beginning With...

I spy With My Little Eye Something Beginning With...

I spy With My Little Eye Something Beginning With...

Y

Valentines day
Valentines day
Z
IT'S A
COLOR ME!
Z...
Z...
Z...
Good JOB
Zzzzzz....